presented to

Barbara xoxo

from

Linda

date

12·04

a lifetime of *Girlfriends*

moments of connection

by Bonnie Jensen

BARBOUR
PUBLISHING

Bonnie would like to acknowledge the generous contribution of
Anita Wiegand to this little book of friendship.
She is not only a joy to work with, but a joy to befriend as well.

© 2004 by Barbour Publishing, Inc.

ISBN 1-59310-365-4

Cover and interior images: Getty Images
Designed by Julie Doll.

Published by Barbour Publishing, Inc., P.O. Box 719, Uhrichsville, Ohio 44683,
www.barbourbooks.com

Our mission is to publish and distribute inspirational products offering exceptional value and biblical encouragement to the masses.

Member of the
Evangelical Christian
Publishers Association

Printed in China.
5 4 3 2 1

It is through kindness and compassion
that hearts connect and friendship begins.

Be kind and compassionate
to one another.

EPHESIANS 4:32 NIV

I may find myself looking in the rearview mirror someday, thinking about what a wonderful blessing my friends have been. Or perhaps I'll be looking ahead, thinking about the path my friendships continue to take. Regardless of the direction I'm looking, I'm so glad my friends are part of the scenery.

I ran into an old friend the other day. After a brief conversation and a little catching up, we promised to keep in touch. . .to "do lunch." Although our busy lives most likely will prevent us from following through, our chance meeting brought back good memories—and the comfort of knowing that it takes only a moment to rekindle a friendship.

conversation

Friends are always friends no matter how far you have to travel back in time.

—*Kellie O'Connor*

comfort

Listen...

A friend is one to whom one may pour
out all the contents of one's heart, chaff
and grain together, knowing that the
gentlest of hands will take and sift it,
keep what is worth keeping, and with a
breath of kindness blow the rest away.

—*Arabian Proverb*

The only way to have
a friend is to be one.

—*Ralph Waldo Emerson*

The one who blesses
others is abundantly
blessed; those who
help others are helped.

PROVERBS 11:25 THE MESSAGE

Don't you wish the friends you haven't seen in a while could be aware of all the moments you think of them and smile?

The greatest sweetener of human life is friendship.
—*Joseph Addison*

Blessed are the
happiness makers;
Blessed are they
that remove friction,
That make the
courses of life smooth.
—Henry Ward Beecher

If I had to choose between a friend and ice cream to ease a tense moment, I would choose a friend because she wouldn't melt under the pressure. Actually, having ice cream with a friend might be the perfect solution!

pressures

True friendship
dwells so deep
that words are
often unnecessary.

intuition

family

Loving thoughts
      and friendly deeds
Watered with blessings,
      grow like weeds.

balancing

There's a lot to balance right now.
Homemaking. Family. Career. Ballet lessons.
Soccer practice. Always keep one hand free.
How else are you going to hold the chocolate. . .
or phone a friend to come to the rescue?

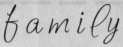

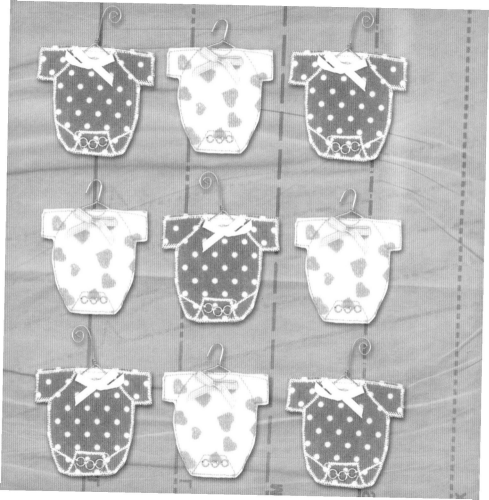

*Friends...
leave lasting
imprints on
our hearts.*
—Anonymous

I sometimes feel I need to
set aside enough time to
write an elaborate, detailed
letter or e-mail to a friend
I haven't spoken to in
a while, when in fact, a
simple "Hello, I've been
thinking about you. . ." is
all her heart really needs
to hear.

Friendship is made up of little things—a pat on the back, an unexpected phone call, a small gift, a note of thanks, a batch of chocolate chip cookies. . .

It takes time for friendship to develop. . .but only a moment for hearts to connect.

Actions, not words, are the true criterion
of the attachment of friends.
    —*George Washington*

In light of our busy schedules, making a lunch date with a friend seems like a monumental challenge. However, after moving mountains to make it happen, the payoff is sweet. Time with a friend is always well spent. . .and the work it takes to make it happen is erased the instant you see each other smile.

What we think we should do for a friend is often exactly what she needs. Kind thoughts that become kind deeds perpetuate a wonderful circle of blessings in our lives.

Kindness

I have a connection with all my
friends. In different ways they have
helped me grow. . .made me laugh. . .
filled my heart with memories. . .
Each one is a special part of a single,
amazing gift—a gift that's been
carefully fashioned by God.

connection

busy, busy, busy

Simplify. Slow down. Breath deeply.
Hide your to-do list. Sit still for ten
minutes. . .and use this quiet time to
thank God for your friends.

Serve one another in love.

GALATIANS 5:13 NIV

Sometimes a brief telephone conversation with a friend is all it takes to make you feel like you've been hugged.

Surround yourself with
people who make you
happy. When you're
smiling on the inside, it
shows on the outside.

Blessed is the influence of one true, loving human soul on another.

—George Eliot

Learn to enjoy
the little things—
there are so many
of them.
—Anonymous

Girlfriends will use any excuse to be together. I remember having a monthly gathering with some of my closest friends. We called it "Bunco," because that was the name of the game we were supposed to be playing. . .but after two years, we hadn't played once. We had too much fun talking and laughing to think about disrupting it with any kind of structured activity!

A handwritten letter to a friend
(on pretty stationery, of course!)
is great therapy. I'm a collector
of fine papers and beautiful
note cards. I find it inspires me
to write my friends more often
because note cards are such a
joy to use—and I know my

letters

friends will be just as pleased
with their charm when they
discover them in their mailboxes.
(It only takes a minute to jot
down your thoughts—thoughts
your friend will cherish for a very
long time.)

thoughts

blessings

May the Lord continually bless you with
heaven's blessings as well as with human joys.
PSALM 128:5 TLB

small talk

It's on those days when everyone you've had
a conversation with is two feet tall or less
that you truly appreciate the voice of a
friend on the telephone!

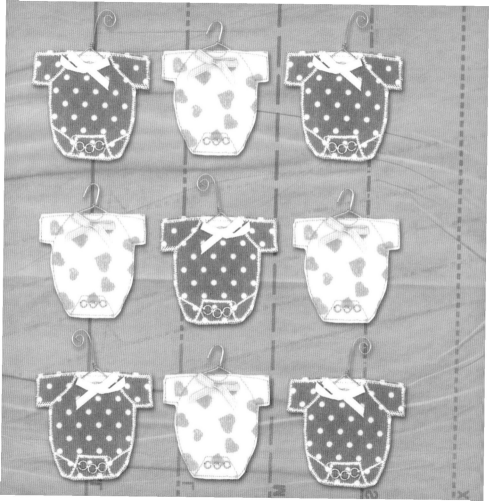

The sweetest
conversation
between friends
is the silent
communication
of their hearts.

A friend loves at all times.

PROVERBS 17:17 NIV

*Encourage one
another and build
each other up.*

1 THESSALONIANS 5:11 NIV

Shopping, chocolate, and friends.
Thank God for life's sweet diversions.

Friends are often full of wonderful little surprises. . . . They always seem to know just what we need without even asking.

There are few things in life as encouraging as the voice of a friend. It's not just the words they speak, but the gentle way they convey them.

*Just one encouraging
word from a friend
can create inspiration
for weeks to come!*

inspiration

*Friendship is a collection
of kindly thoughts,
of love-rich seeds,
of heartfelt words,
and caring deeds.*
        —Roy Lessin

heartfelt words

relating

It's great when your girlfriends are going through the same things you are. . .wearing all the same hats, facing all the same issues. It allows you to connect on a deeper level and completely relate to each other's urge to have "no hat" days.

The annual "sending of Christmas cards" is a great way to reconnect with friends. Even if you've gone an entire year without communicating, it's the perfect opportunity to let them know that time and distance cannot lessen the value of the friendship you share.

*A friend
listens with
her heart.*

Friends have a special
talent of reading between
the lines.

When it comes to raising a family and keeping balance between work and home, friends are a great source for much-needed advice. (We can learn so much from each other!)

If you're having a bad day and the chocolate is all gone, call a friend.

A friend is someone who
reaches for your hand but
touches your heart.
—from *The Little Prince*
by Antoine de Saint-Exupery

Friends. . .
talk together,
cry together,
pray together.

together

Surround yourself
with friends!
They are the support
system of life.

support

crying

One of the comforts of friendship is knowing
you can call a friend anytime—day or night—
for empathy, advice, or a shoulder to cry on.

dieting

A true friend is someone who'll skip dessert
because you're on a diet.

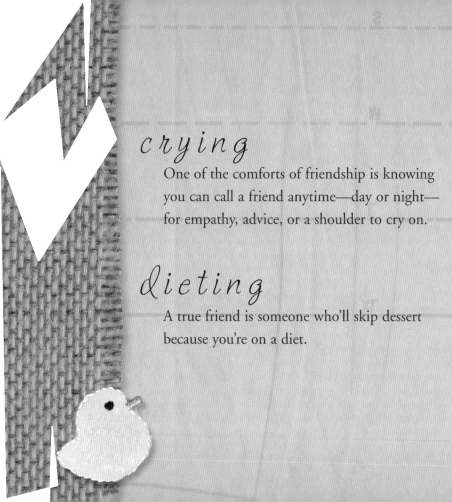

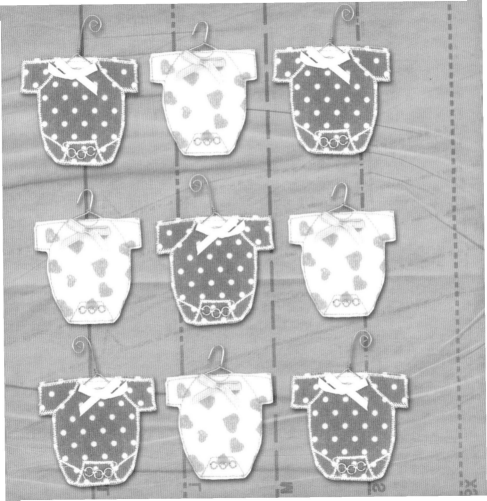

Friends have all things in common.

—Greek Proverb

It is sometimes
enough for a
friend to just
"be there" and
listen without
saying a word.

Friends see you differently
than others do. . . . God must
have equipped them with a "positive
light" lens to look through.

A real friend will tell you if you
have lipstick on your teeth. . .then
compliment you on the color.

Friends love through all kinds of weather.
PROVERBS 17:17 THE MESSAGE

The road to a
friend's house
is never long.
—*Dutch Proverb*

Friendships keep us
grounded; they rarely
allow us to stray from
being true to ourselves.

true

Friends have a way
of calming fears
and restoring hope.

calming

influence

My best friend is the one who brings out
the best in me.

—*Henry Ford*

dreams

Friends. . .they cherish each other's hopes.
They are kind to each other's dreams.

—*Henry David Thoreau*

Friendship is a sheltering tree.
—Samuel Taylor Coleridge

Friendship
seems to find
me when I need
it the most.

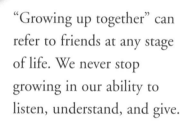

"Growing up together" can refer to friends at any stage of life. We never stop growing in our ability to listen, understand, and give.

I adore simple pleasures.
They are the last refuge of the complex.
—Oscar Wilde

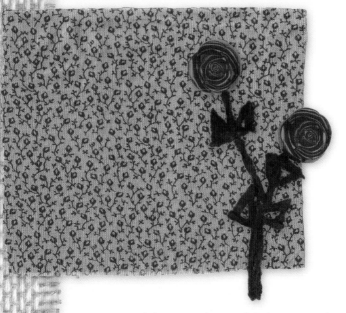

The most beautiful discovery that true
friends can make is that they can grow
separately without growing apart.

—*Elizabeth Foley*

I have a friend I love to laugh with. Her giggle makes me laugh, and my giggle makes her laugh. There are also times when we laugh so hard we don't make any sound at all. We think it's the greatest form of "quiet time"—proven to soothe everything from a bad day to a broken heart.

*A cheerful
heart does good
like medicine.*

PROVERBS 17:22 TLB

happy hearts

From quiet homes and first beginning,
  Out to the undiscovered ends,
There's nothing worth the wear of winning,
  But laughter and the love of friends.
    —*J. D. Bellay*

laughter

life's trials

Great times to be a friend to a friend:

When all her possessions are in cardboard
  boxes, and she's dreading the thought of
  fast food again. . .
When the baby has arrived but her energy
  hasn't returned. . .
When she's been too sick to fulfill her role as
  a domestic goddess. . .
When her heart is aching, and she's in need
  of tissues, chocolate, a sympathetic ear, or
  any combination of the three.

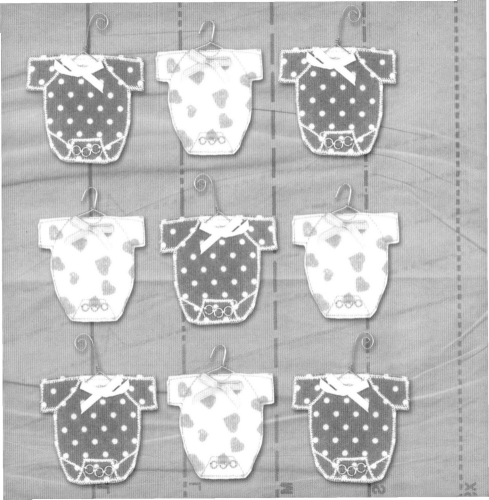

Long years apart
can make no breach
a second cannot fill.
—Emily Dickinson

I'm glad there's no limit on
how many friends we can
welcome into our lives.
God created our hearts with
the capacity to hold as many
as we want!

Friends share lots of simple pleasures—but a mutual affection for chocolate is one of the most enjoyable.

How many M&M's does it take to have a good, long
conversation with a friend? As many as the children want. . . .

Meeting a new friend is God's way of
asking us to open our hearts a little
wider, make a little more room to be
thoughtful, and take a little more time
to express His love.

Do not protect yourself by a fence, but rather by your friends.
—Czech Proverb

The ties of friendship are
strengthened by adversity
and joy. . .tears and
laughter. . .two spoons and
one hot fudge sundae.

ice cream

Even on the
busiest of days,
friends make time
for each other.

phone calls

connected hearts

God created our hearts. . .
He connects them too.

One of the most
wonderful
characteristics of
friendship is
its ability to
remain constant
and valuable
during periods of
dormancy.

The moment friends
communicate or
reunite, they are at
once reminded of
each other's worth—
and their hearts find
an immediate and
familiar connection.

Friends find joy in the
pleasure of each other's
company, the sound of
each other's laughter,
the fulfillment of each
other's dreams.

Invest heavily in your friendships.
You will be repaid in kind.